CW00408313

THE L

VII

TIPS

ANDREW LANGLEY

THE LITTLE BOOK OF VINEGAR TIPS

ANDREW LANGLEY

A.
Absolute Press

First published in Great Britain in 2008 by
Absolute Press
Scarborough House, 29 James Street West
Bath BA1 2BT, England
Phone 44 (0) 1225 316013 **Fax** 44 (0) 1225 445836
E-mail info@absolutepress.co.uk
Web www.absolutepress.co.uk

A catalogue record of this book is available from the British Library

ISBN 13: 9781904573920

Printed and bound in China by 1010

‘Salt it, temper it up with vinegar,
and serve it forth’

**Guillaume Tirel (1310–1395),
cook to Charles V of France**

1

Vinegar is simply **alcohol which has been converted into acetic acid.** It has been important to us throughout history because it kills many harmful microbes. This makes it both a disinfecting agent and a preservative liquid for food.

2

Wine vinegar

is made, naturally enough, from grape juice which has been fermented with yeast. Just as obviously, it **has** a winey character, giving it more **buttery and savoury flavours and aromas** than others. Use wine vinegar in meat sauces, as the basis for dressings, and to accompany preserved fruits.

3

Strangely, **vinegar** molecules have fat-like characteristics. They will therefore absorb a lot more chemical traces than water. In layman's terms, this means that vinegar **is very good at picking up aromas and flavours,** especially from herbs and spices.

4

Vinegar has a higher boiling point than water.

The main value of this for cooks is that boiling will make it more concentrated. So high quality vinegar is ideal for adding flavour to sauces and glazes – though in moderation.

5

Make your own vinegar #1: the right microbes.

Wild microbes will turn alcohol to vinegar, but may produce unpleasant flavours. Instead, start with a 'mother' – the cloudy stuff at the bottom of a bottle of good active commercial vinegar. This will create a consistent and tasty result.

6

Cider vinegar is made from apple juice fermented with yeast.

Brown in colour, it often has a pleasing suggestion of farmyards. Use it for pickling and for stewing meat and fruits. Cider vinegar also contains many trace elements and has an amazing number of medicinal uses.

7

How strong is your vinegar?

Vinegars vary widely in strength

(levels of acetic acid), and this will have a bearing on your cooking. Wine vinegars may have 7% or more, whereas rice vinegars may have less than 4%. The percentage should be stated on the label.

8

Malt vinegar is made from something very like beer

- the fermented wash from malted barley. Its strong, coarse flavour cuts through fats, making it a perfect dressing for fish and chips. Malt vinegar will never be haute cuisine, but is fine for pickling onions and making hearty preserves such as piccalilli.

9

What is **non-brewed condiment?** This liquid, found in most fish and chip shops, is a totally artificial vinegar substitute. It consists of acetic acid (made from industrial alcohol), water, flavourings and colourings, and **should be avoided wherever possible.**

10

Make your own vinegar #2: a mother is born.

If you don't fancy the dregs (see Tip 5), create a 'mother' yourself. Mix equal quantities of good quality vinegar and alcohol (preferably wine or cider) in a jar. Cover with muslin and leave in a warm place for a fortnight. The scum which forms on top is the 'mother'.

11

Rice vinegar is a crucial ingredient in sushi rice. Wash, soak and steam 300g (10oz) sushi rice, and spread out on a dish. Then heat 37ml (2fl oz) of rice vinegar with 1½ tablespoons of sugar and a pinch of salt until mixed. Allow to cool and them fold gently into the rice.

12

Proper balsamic vinegar is in a league of its own. Made from cooked grape must, it is matured for at least ten years and has an unmatched richness. But beware: there are many cheap imitations (good enough for cooking). Only bottles marked '*Tradizionale di Modena*', numbered and sealed, are genuine.

13

Balsamic vinegar goes sensationally well with strawberries and tomatoes.

Sprinkle sparingly on a bowl of strawberries or on a salad of good sweet sliced tomatoes. No other adornment is needed.

14

Here's piquant combination –

salmon with radicchio and balsamic vinegar.

Wrap peppered salmon steaks in blanched radicchio leaves and steam for about 15 minutes. Before serving, dress with olive oil and a few drops of balsamico.

15

Make your own vinegar #3: mixing and maturing. Put your wine or cider (or even beer) in a clean jar. Add the aforesaid dregs or the ‘mother’ (Tip 10). Cover with muslin and leave in a warm place, such as an airing cupboard. Mature over at least a month, checking the taste occasionally.

16

Cider vinegar and pork go together like apples and pigs.

Spread mustard on 4 pork chops and sauté both sides in oil. Add 250ml (8fl oz) cider and a little brown sugar, cook a little longer then remove the chops. Stir in 2 tablespoons of cider vinegar, reduce and pour over the chops. Cook on for another 5 minutes.

17

Sardines *'en escabeche'* will keep – and grow in flavour – for a week.

Gently fry floured sardines in olive oil, then dry and lay in a dish. Simmer a marinade of 3 parts good red wine vinegar to 1 part water, plus bay leaves, coriander seeds, garlic and ½ teaspoon of sugar. When cool, pour over the fish and pop in the fridge.

18

Vinegar pie is tastier than it sounds.

Line a 9-inch tin with pastry and bake blind. Add 450g (1lb) of sugar and 55g (2oz) of flour to 450ml (16fl oz) of boiling water and cook for 5 minutes. Away from heat, whisk in 2 beaten eggs. Back on the heat, beat in 6 tablespoons cider vinegar and a dash of Limoncello. Cool and refrigerate till set.

19

Vinaigrette is the simplest of all salad dressings.

Mix 5 parts good olive oil to 1 part good wine vinegar and season with sea salt and ground pepper. Sounds easy, but beware. The two most common faults are: bad quality vinegar, or too much vinegar.

20

Make your own vinegar #4: diluting and storing. If your vinegar seems too strong, add a little water. Once you are happy with the flavour, decant the liquid into a clean bottle through a paper coffee filter. Seal with a cork (the vinegar will corrode a metal top).

21

Fruit vinegars are, strictly speaking, **made from fruit wines.** The most popular include apple, raspberry, quince, pineapple, coconut and date. Try experimenting with your own fruit wines, using the same procedure as for home-made wine vinegar.

22

Shallot vinegar is an instant accompaniment for raw oysters or mussels. Simply mix together 50ml (2fl oz) of red wine vinegar with the same amount of red wine, and add a couple of shallots chopped very fine.

23

Pickle **baby turnips in vinegar.**

Fry 1kg (2lb) of cleaned and trimmed baby turnips in oil until browned all over. Add chopped garlic, 4 tablespoons of red wine vinegar and seasoning. Cook for another couple of minutes, then cool and serve with a nice glass of Manzanilla sherry.

24

Syracusan Tuna is another **magical fish and vinegar combo.** Make slits in a chunk of tuna and insert garlic slivers, cloves and coriander seeds. Sauté sliced onion in oil, brown the fish, then add a tin of tomatoes. After 20 minutes, add oregano and 3 tablespoons of white wine vinegar. Cook 15 minutes more, slice and serve.

25

Many **marinades feature vinegar very heavily.**

Here's one for chicken. In a deep dish, combine 4 tablespoons of red wine vinegar, a garlic clove, fresh rosemary, lemon zest and seasoning. Immerse one free range chicken, cut into 8 portions and skinned, for at least 2 hours before cooking.

26

Sherry vinegar makes an incomparable onion marmalade.

Gently brown 900g (2lb) sliced onions in 175g (6oz) butter and 200g (7oz) sugar. Season and cook slowly for 30 minutes, stirring occasionally. Add 150ml (5fl oz) sherry vinegar plus 300ml (10fl oz) red wine and cook another 30 minutes before cooling and bottling.

27

Vinegar and honey are a venerable pairing. Make a dressing by combining 4 tablespoons of red wine vinegar with 2 tablespoons each of Greek honey and olive oil. Season judiciously. Use this with a salad of thinly sliced cucumber, chervil and olives.

28

Yet another

vinegar sauce perfect for fish (or chicken).

Whizz up 150g ($5\frac{1}{2}$oz) blanched almonds in a processor. Add 3 tablespoons of water and 2 slices of stale white bread (also soaked in water), then olive oil and water until smooth and just runny. Finally mix in sherry vinegar to taste plus some capers.

29

For the best spicy apple chutney, peel, core and chop 2kg (4lb) of apples. Simmer with 4 chopped onions, 450g (1lb) of sultanas, 900g (2lb) of sugar, teaspoons of mustard seed, ground ginger, cinnamon, ground cloves and 1.2 litres (2 pints) of cider vinegar. Cook, stirring, for at least 1½ hours, then cool and bottle.

30

Raspberry vinegar can be used **on salads and grills.** Put 900g (2lb) washed raspberries in a glass bowl and lightly crush. Pour over 580ml (1 pint) red wine vinegar, cover with a cloth and leave for 7 days. Strain through muslin. Add sugar if you wish. Boil for 10 minutes and bottle when cool.

31

Souse herrings in vinegar to make rollmops.

Clean, split and fillet 8 medium herrings. Soak them for 3 hours in salty brine. After this, rinse the fish in vinegar, roll them up and pack into a jar with bay leaves and juniper berries. Boil up cider vinegar with pickling spices, cool and pour into the jars. Leave for two days before sampling.

32

Be choosy about the vinegar you use for pickles and chutneys.

Malt vinegar is fine for the rumbustious stuff (such as pickled onions), but reserve cider or even wine vinegars for more delicate preserves (such as pickled fruits). They do make a difference to the taste.

33

Flavour your own pickling vinegar

– it's better than buying ready-made. Experiment with combinations of spices, from coriander and cloves to allspice and cardamom, or try using just one for a pure character. Add to the vinegar, bring to the boil, allow to cool and strain.

34

Pickled onions deserve care.

They should be

small and sweet.

Blanch them (skins on) briefly in boiling water. Then dunk in cold water and peel them. Salt them well and leave in a bowl overnight. Next day, rinse and dry them and pack them in jars. Top up with a nice sweet cider vinegar and sugar mix.

35

Prevent cooking vegetables from discolouring.

Pop a judicious amount (a teaspoonful) of white vinegar into the cooking water. This is especially helpful with potatoes, or with vegetables which stain easily, such as globe artichokes.

36

Flavour white wine vinegar with tarragon.

Simply pack a clean bottle with fresh tarragon leaves, top up with vinegar and cork. Leave in a sunny spot for two weeks, shaking each day. Strain and re-bottle. Many other herbs benefit from this treatment, notably dill, sage and hyssop.

37

Mint and vinegar syrup is a delicious drink from ancient Persia.

Boil together 250ml (8fl oz) of water and 250g (8oz) of sugar for 10 minutes. Add the juice of 1 lemon and 4 tablespoons of white wine vinegar. Boil another 10 minutes, adding a handful of mint leaves. Cool, strain and serve very cold (with ice).

38

Have a

vinegar spray handy in the kitchen.

In a spray bottle, mix equal parts of vinegar and water. Give a quick squirt when you wipe tables or worktops, or when you clean high chairs or other baby equipment. It will keep harmful bacteria at bay.

39

The **acetic acid**

in vinegar makes it

a potent dissolver of limescale.

Rub neat vinegar over shower heads and bath taps. Leave it overnight in your lavatory bowl or (diluted) in your electric kettle or coffee maker and it will eat away the lime.

40

Got a CD or DVD that sticks?

Put a sparing amount of white vinegar onto a soft cloth and wipe very gently over the business side. This will get rid of grease and other gunk. Make sure the disk is dry before you use it again.

41

Freeze a tray of **vinegar ice cubes.** Once a week, **pop a couple in the dishwasher** just before a cycle. They will keep the machine both stain- and odour-free. You can also use the cubes with a clothes wash.

42

Vinegar will deter pesky kitchen insects.

Spray some round doorways, pedal bins and compost buckets. Ants and fruit flies, among other pests, dislike the smell and will stay away.

43

Remember that **vinegar is** an acidic liquid. It is therefore **perfect for treating nettle and other plant stings,** which are generally alkaline. Apply the vinegar to the affected area with a cloth or cotton wool.

44

Neat (and strong) **white vinegar will kill many broad-leaved weeds** – without leaving any harmful residues. Spray it on concrete or gravel paths every fortnight and watch the leaves shrivel.

45

Plagued by a

smelly fridge? Wipe out

the inside sparingly with soapy water, then

with neat white vinegar.

Dry with a tea towel. Keep a little dish of vinegar always in the fridge to keep it deodorized.

46

At the first sign of **flu or a sore throat,**

mix yourself a glass of

hot cider vinegar and honey.

Put a good slug of vinegar in the glass, top up with hot water, and stir in a generous teaspoon of honey. Repeat every few hours.

47

Cider vinegar is a legendary health food.

It contains an almost unrivalled range of minerals and trace elements, notably potassium, as well as vitamins (including C and E). Take a teaspoon every day in water to combat (so it's claimed) arthritis, high cholesterol and high blood pressure.

48

Gargling with vinegar will help to control gum disease

and give your teeth a deep down clean. It will also get rid of bad breath. Always remember to rinse with water afterwards, as neat vinegar may corrode tooth enamel.

49

Relax in a vinegar bath:

it cleans and softens as it soaks. Add about 1 litre (2 pints) of cider or white wine vinegar to your bathwater. Stir in some mint leaves, rose petals or camomile for extra luxury.

50

Thrill the kids with **a vinegar volcano.** Put an empty plastic bottle on a tray. Fill most of it with warm water. Add (in this order) 2 drops of red colouring, 6 drops of detergent and 2 tablespoons of baking soda. Now slowly pour in some white vinegar – and stand back.

Andrew Langley

Andrew Langley is a knowledgeable food and drink writer. Among his formative influences he lists a season picking grapes in Bordeaux, several years of raising sheep and chickens in Wiltshire and two decades drinking his grandmother's tea. He has written books on a number of Scottish and Irish whisky distilleries and is the editor of the highly regarded anthology of the writings of the legendary Victorian chef Alexis Soyer.

THE LITTLE BOOK OF
BARBECUE
TIPS
ANDREW LANGLEY

THE LITTLE BOOK OF
BEER
TIPS
ANDREW LANGLEY

THE LITTLE BOOK OF
HERB
TIPS
WILLIAM FORTT

THE LITTLE BOOK OF
POKER
TIPS

THE LITTLE BOOK OF
GARDENING
TIPS
WILLIAM FORTT

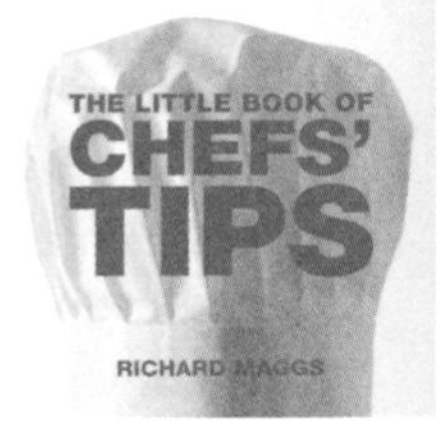
THE LITTLE BOOK OF
CHEFS'
TIPS
RICHARD MAGGS

THE LITTLE BOOK OF
SPICE
TIPS
ANDREW LANGLEY

THE LITTLE BOOK OF
GOLF
TIPS
PETER FRENCH

THE LITTLE BOOK OF
TIPS
SERIES

THE LITTLE BOOK OF
CHEESE
TIPS
ANDREW LANGLEY

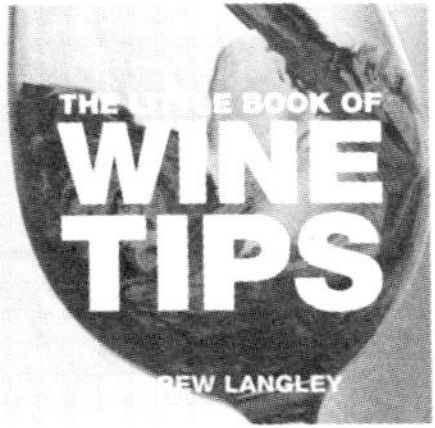
WINE
TIPS

THE LITTLE BOOK OF
AGA
TIPS²
RICHARD MAGGS

THE LITTLE BOOK OF
COFFEE
TIPS
ANDREW LANGLEY

THE LITTLE BOOK OF
TEA
TIPS
ANDREW LANGLEY

THE LITTLE BOOK OF
AGA
TIPS³
RICHARD MAGGS

THE LITTLE BOOK OF
AGA
TIPS
RICHARD MAGGS

THE LITTLE BOOK OF
CHRISTMAS
AGA
TIPS
RICHARD MAGGS

THE LITTLE BOOK OF
RAYBURN
TIPS
RICHARD MAGGS

THE LITTLE BOOK OF
BRIDGE
TIPS

THE LITTLE BOOK OF
CHESS
TIPS

THE LITTLE BOOK OF
FISHING
TIPS
MICK DEVENISH

THE LITTLE BOOK OF
GREEN
TIPS
WILLIAM FORTT

THE LITTLE BOOK OF
KITTEN
TIPS
ANDREW LANGLEY

MARMITE
THE LITTLE BOOK OF
MARMITE
TIPS

THE LITTLE BOOK OF
PUPPY
TIPS
ANDREW LANGLEY

THE LITTLE BOOK OF
WHISKY
TIPS
ANDREW LANGLEY

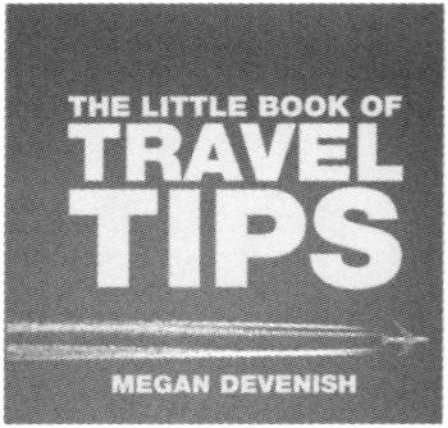
THE LITTLE BOOK OF
TRAVEL
TIPS
MEGAN DEVENISH